Wrong!

Jane O'Boyle is a writer who lives in Charleston, South Carolina

Wrong!

The Biggest Mistakes and Miscalculations Ever Made by People Who Should Have Known Better

JANE O'BOYLE

For Mr Right

With special thanks to
Janis Donnaud, Jennifer Moore
and Clare Ferraro

First published in Great Britain in 2000 by
Michael O'Mara Books Limited
9 Lion Yard
Tremadoc Road
London SW4 7NQ

Wrong!: The Biggest Mistakes and Miscalculations Ever Made by People Who Should Have Known Better by Jane O'Boyle.

A CIP catalogue record for this book is available from the British Library

ISBN 1-85479-525-2

1 3 5 7 9 10 8 6 4 2

Designed and typeset by SX Composing DTP, Rayleigh, Essex
Printed and bound by Cox & Wyman Ltd, Reading, Berks

Introduction!

The errors of a wise man make your rule
Rather than the perfections of a fool.

– William Blake

A man should never be ashamed to own that he has been in the wrong, which is but saying, in other words, that he is wiser today than he was yesterday.

– Jonathan Swift

William Blake and Jonathan Swift were rarely wrong. The rest of us, however, often prove fallible in our opinions and observations, even about things we know very well. Sometimes, we even emphasize our boldness by adding wagers like 'I'll eat my hat!' and 'or my name isn't Richard Nixon!' This proves that we are, at least, artful in our moments of bombastic artlessness. And thus, perhaps, easier to forgive. We might try to forget about our lapse in judgement and move on, but there is frequently someone else who finds it too momentous to let it pass without an 'I told you so!' or handing you that old beret with a knife and fork.

There was a time when being right all the time was not a good thing. Galileo has his finger on the truth when he invented the thermometer, the proportional compass, the telescope, and then nailed down planetary motion (although we know he too made a couple of mistakes along the way). For his successes, a papal Inquisition excommunicated Galileo from the Catholic Church and barred him from doing further scientific work. Back then, this was the equivalent of a massive tax audit while losing your job, but even worse.

Being right is not always best, for other reasons too. When Babe Ruth was pulled over for driving the wrong way down a one-way street, he replied, 'But I'm only going one way.' Babe was not wrong, technically. Nor do we feel that Babe should have even known better. He was revered as a terrific baseball player, not as a safe driver. Had Babe hit a home run and run around the bases the wrong way, clockwise, then we could say he should have known better. Between Babe Ruth and Galileo, however, two rights can make a wrong.

What follows is a compendium of 'famous last words' and anecdotes to warm the heart of anyone who has been known to screw up, big time. Some of these prognosticators faltered into oblivion. Others went on to greater glory because they risked being wrong – again – and were not. Take pride in those instances when you are wrong. They are so rare, after all. And no one achieved success without being wrong, at least once.

Music and Movies

Many people made a bad decision during the course of their careers. Fortunately for some, in the entertainment industry one person's mistake is always someone else's lucky break.

'People will tire of talkers. Talking is no substitute for the good acting we had in silent pictures.'

– Thomas Alva Edison, 1925, on new movies with sound.

'Talking pictures are merely chirping tintypes.'

– *Variety*, 1925.

'Who the hell wants to hear actors talk?'

– Harry Warner, Warner Bros, 1926.

'Novelty is always welcome, but talking pictures are just a fad.'

– MGM movie producer Irving Thalberg, 1927.

'Every woman is frightened of a mouse.'

– MGM head Louis B. Mayer in 1926, to a young cartoonist named Walt Disney. Mayer scoffed at the notion that a rodent would ever be popular in movies. Rejected by MGM, Walt and Roy Disney distributed Mickey Mouse movies on their own. By 1932, the Mickey Mouse fan club had a million members. The Disney Company currently has annual revenues in the neighbourhood of $22 billion.

'Forget bus pictures. People don't want 'em. MGM and Universal just made two bus operas and they both stink.'

– Columbia Pictures chief Harry Cohn's advice in 1934 to director Frank Capra, who was considering making a movie of a story he'd just read in *Cosmopolitan* magazine. But Capra went ahead anyway, although he changed the title from *Night Bus* to *It Happened One Night*.

'I've just finished the worst picture of the year.'

– Actress Claudette Colbert to her friends, upon completing the filming of Capra's *It Happened One Night* with Clark Gable. When it was released, the film was a huge success and won five Oscars, including Best Actress, Best Actor, Best Screenplay, Best Director, and Best Picture.

Howard Hawks had a hard time casting the role of Hildy Johnson in the screen comedy *His Girl Friday*. Ginger Rogers, Janet Gaynor, Jean Arthur, Claudette Colbert, and Carole Lombard all turned it down. The role eventually went to an unknown actress named Rosalind Russell, and it made her famous.

The producers of *The Wizard of Oz* planned for W.C. Fields to play the title role. Some say money was an issue, others say Fields simply turned it down so he could write the screenplay for *You Can't Cheat an Honest Man*. Frank Morgan replaced Fields.

'I'm just glad it'll be Clark Gable who's falling on his face, and not Gary Cooper.'

– Gary Cooper, after declining the lead role in *Gone With the Wind,* which became one of the largest-grossing films of all time.

'It will be the biggest bust in town.'

– Moviemaker Jack Warner about *Gone With the Wind,* in an attempt to dissuade Olivia de Havilland from playing the role of Melanie Wilkes.

'Anyone can moan and grunt. I will not be a babbling idiot for anybody. I need a part where I can *act*.'

– Movie star Bela Lugosi, turning down the monster role in *Frankenstein*. Boris Karloff, an unknown forty-four-year-old actor, said he would be 'delighted' to take the part. *Frankenstein* made Karloff a household name – an even bigger star than Lugosi.

Twelve years later, Lugosi changed his tune and starred in one of several sequels, *Frankenstein Meets the Wolf Man,* but, by then, his career had hit the skids.

'As you know, I feel strongly that *The Maltese Falcon* . . . is not an important picture.'

– Movie star George Raft, in a letter to studio chief Jack Warner. Raft, a huge box office star, didn't want to play Sam Spade because first-time director John Huston had little experience. Raft got his wish, and instead he made a completely forgettable movie called *Manpower,* about a group of men who worked on high-voltage lines. Meanwhile, his part in *The Maltese Falcon* went to Humphrey Bogart, who became a star, right along with the new director, John Huston.

In fact, *The Maltese Falcon* was such an enormous success that it enabled Bogart to clinch the part of Rick Blaine in *Casablanca,* a role that George Raft had badly wanted. The following year, Raft had one more chance to regain his box office stature. He was offered the starring role in Billy Wilder's suspense thriller *Double Indemnity*. But, alas, George turned it down. With unknown Fred MacMurray in the lead role opposite Barbara Stanwyck, *Double Indemnity* became a landmark classic.

Actress Hedy Lamarr was very smart. She invented a frequency-switching torpedo-guidance system which eventually formed the basis for secure American military communications. When it came to choosing movie roles, however, she was not so canny. In 1941, Lamarr turned down the starring role in *Casablanca,* because she didn't want to work with an unfinished script. The following year, she also turned down the lead in *Gaslight*. These two roles went to newcomer Ingrid Bergman, who became an instant star in *Casablanca* and won an Academy Award for her role in *Gaslight.* Lamarr did not win any wards for *The Heavenly Body* or *White Cargo,* the movies she made instead of *Casablanca* and *Gaslight.*

'No legs, no jokes, no chance.'

– Producer Mike Todd in 1943, at a preview of Rodgers and Hammerstein's *Oklahoma!*, which became one of the most successful theatrical productions of all time.

Montgomery Clift turned down *Sunset Boulevard* in 1950, because he didn't think audiences would believe his love scenes with a woman thirty-five years his senior. Fred MacMurray also turned down the part. William Holden starred in this Billy Wilder classic with Gloria Swanson, and it helped make him a major star.

In the original opening scenes of *Sunset Boulevard,* a roomful of cadavers take turns telling how they died, until eventually Joe Gillis (Holden) tells us the story in flashback about his affair with Norma Desmond. The preview audiences in Evanston, Illinois, found the cavaders' voice-overs hilarious and laughed uproariously. Since this response was not appropriate to the story, Billy Wilder spent another six months reshooting a new opening, with Holden's body discovered in the swimming pool, as Gillis alone narrates his story.

'You ain't going nowhere . . . You ought to go back to driving a truck!'

– Jim Denny, Grand Ole Opry manager, to struggling musician Elvis Presley, after his first Opry show in 1954. Elvis was also rejected by Arthur Godfrey's *Talent Scouts.*

'You're gonna make a little black-and-white film, no one's ever going to hear of it, you're gonna think you're a star and you're not gonna be a star.'

– Spencer Tracy to actor Ernest Borgnine in 1954, while they were filming *Bad Day at Black Rock.* Borgnine was, once again, playing a villain, but had an opportunity to play the lead in a small film by an unknown named Paddy Chayevsky. In spite of Tracy's advice, Borgnine took the part. And Borgnine beat fellow nominee Spencer Tracy to win the 1955 Academy Award for Best Actor for his role in *Marty.*

'I have just come from the Actors' Studio where I saw Marilyn Monroe. She had no girdle on, her ass was hanging out. She is a disgrace to the industry.'

– Joan Crawford, 1955

Eva Marie Saint turned down the starring role in *The Three Faces of Eve* to make *Raintree County*. A new actress named Joanne Woodward took the part, for which she won the 1957 Academy Award as Best Actress.

The Moonglows had a 1958 hit with their song 'The Ten Commandments of Love'. Few fans noticed that the song lists only nine commandments.

'I'll be damned if I'll spend two years of my life out in the desert on some f—g camel!'

– Marlon Brando in 1962, turning down the starring role in David Lean's *Lawrence of Arabia.* Brando instead spent a year in Tahiti, for a remake of *Mutiny on the Bounty.* After actor Albert Finney also turned down the role of T.E. Lawrence, Lean chose an unknown named Peter O'Toole, who won an Oscar nomination for his performance. Brando's *Mutiny* was a flop that nearly bankrupted MGM.

'We don't like their sound, they sound too much like the Shadows, and guitar music is on the way out anyway.'

– Decca Records producers, about the Beatles, January 1962. This discouraging criticism prompted the Beatles to discuss breaking up before they recorded their first record. EMI gave them one last try by releasing 'Love Me Do' in October 1962. It was an immediate hit. Within months, Decca Records had been folded into MCA. The Beatles became much, much bigger than the Shadows.

'The band's OK but, if I were you, I'd get rid of the singer with the tyre-tread lips.'

– BBC radio producer, on rejecting the Rolling Stones at a 1963 audition.

In 1965, Kirk Douglas turned down the role of Kid Shelleen in *Cat Ballou,* following the advice of his agent. Lee Marvin went on to win an Academy Award for his performance in the role.

'Rock 'n roll is the most brutal, ugly, desperate, vicious form of expression it has been my misfortune to hear.'

– Frank Sinatra, whom we love, but his later renditions of 'Bad, Bad Leroy Brown' and 'You Are the Sunshine of My Life' almost force us to agree with him.

Doris Day turned down the starring role of Mrs Robinson in *The Graduate*. It didn't suit her image. The role was eventually played by Anne Bancroft, who was twenty years younger than the character. So what did Doris do instead? Does a spy thriller called *Caprice* ring a bell?

In 1969, Elvis Presley was looking for a more serious movie role. But he turned down a starring role in *Midnight Cowboy,* which went to Jon Voight, and spent that year filming *Change of Habit* with Mary Tyler Moore instead. Since it was about a doctor and a nun in the ghetto, that qualified as being more serious. Which would Mary choose: the lamb of God, or the mutton-chop sideburns? *Change of Habit* was Presley's least successful movie. *Midnight Cowboy* won several Academy Awards, including Best Picture, and made a star out of Jon Voight.

'I think this kind of garish stuff is over. Forget the makeup, and do it my way.'

– Neil Bogart of Warner Bros, to Gene Simmons and Paul Stanley, members of the band Kiss, in their early years. The band found huge success in spite of the garish stuff.

In 1976, Barbra Streisand desperately wanted Elvis Presley as her leading man in *A Star is Born*. But Elvis didn't want to appear as a rock-and-roll has-been, and he certainly didn't want to take direction from Streisand. Plus, his manager, Colonel Parker, hated the idea. The part went to mellow Kris Kristofferson instead. And, as life imitates art, the real-life addicted and faded star died a year later.

The Grammy Award for Best New Artist of 1989 was awarded to Rob Pilatus and Fab Morvan, also known as Milli Vanilli. This award emboldened the pair to demand a higher royalty rate for their second album. Instead, their producer pulled the plug on them, and revealed to the world that their voices had not been used on the first album. The Grammy committee might accept lip-synching on a video, but not on a musical recording. Their Grammy Award was rescinded.

'Don't no girl wanna give Heavy D. no p—.'

– Producer Russell Simmons to Andre Harrell, suggesting a little-known overweight rapper named Heavy D. would never appeal to music fans. This prompted Harrell to leave Simmons's Rush Management and start Uptown Records, where Heavy D. earned many a platinum record, and probably some other things too.

SCIENCE AND TECHNOLOGY

Mark Twain said that the greatest of all the inventions was accident. More than anything, innovation in technology relies on the lessons of human error and the process of elimination. Nevertheless, there have been some grandiloquent whoppers.

'Drill for oil? You mean, drill into the ground to try to find oil? You're crazy.'

– Professional drillers in 1859, when Edwin L. Drake tried to enlist their services.

'The "telephone" has too many shortcomings to be seriously considered as a means of communication. The device is inherently of no value to us.'

– Western Union internal memo, 1876

'That's an amazing invention, but who would ever want to use one of them?'

– US President Rutherford B. Hayes in 1876, after experimenting with a new-fangled telephone in a trial conversation between Washington and Philadelphia.

'Heavier-than-air flying machines are impossible.'

– Lord Kelvin, President of the Royal Society, 1895. A few years later, this British physicist also declared, 'X-rays are a hoax.

'It can be exploited for a certain time as a scientific curiosity, but apart from that it has no commercial value whatsoever.'

– Auguste Lumière, 1895, on his own invention, cinematography.

'Shows no promise.'

– Munich Technical Institute rejecting a young applicant named Albert Einstein in 1898.

'Everything that can be invented, has been invented.'

– Charles Duell, commissioner of the US Patent Office, 1899.

'Flight by machines heavier than air is unpractical and insignificant, if not utterly impossible.'

– Amercian astronomer Simon Newcomb, in 1902 (eighteen months before the Wright brothers' first flight at Kitty Hawk).

'I cannot imagine any condition which would cause a ship to founder. . . . Modern shipbuilding has gone beyond that.'

– Captain Edward J. Smith in 1906, a few years before he commanded the *Titanic*, which hit an iceberg and foundered on its maiden voyage.

'The aeroplane will never fly.'

– Lord Haldane, Minister of War, Britain, 1907 (four years after Kitty Hawk).

'In fifteen years, more electricity will be sold for electric vehicles than for light.'

– Thomas Edison in 1910, who was off by at least a hundred years.

'Aeroplanes are interesting toys but of no military value.'

– General (later Maréchal) Ferdinand Foch, professor of strategy at France's École Supérieure de Guerre, 1911.

'I can accept the theory of relativity as little as I can accept the existence of atoms and other such dogmas.'

– Viennese physicist Ernst Mach, famous for his landmark work on inertia and measuring sound, in 1913.

'The cinema is little more than a fad. It's canned drama. What audiences really want to see is flesh and blood on the stage.'

– Charlie Chaplin, 1916.

'Most improbable and more like one of Jules Verne's stories.'

– British Admiral Sir Compton Dombile in 1914, referring to the concept of submarine warfare, as suggested in a recent story by Sir Arthur Conan Doyle.

'The energy produced by the atom is a very poor kind of thing. Anyone who expects a source of power from the transformation of these atoms is talking moonshine.'

– Lord (Ernest P.) Rutherford, Cambridge physics professor, after he split the atom for the first time in 1933.

'Professor Goddard does not know the relation between action and reaction and the need to have something better than a vacuum against which to react. He seems to lack the basic knowledge ladled out daily in high schools.'

– *New York Times* editorial in 1920, on Robert Goddard's revolutionary rocket work, disputing Goddard's claim that rockets could function in a vacuum. The newspaper retracted this editorial forty-nine years later, when *Apollo 11* proved Goddard's theories to be correct in 1969: 'The *Times* regrets [its] error.'

'This fellow Charles Lindbergh will never make it. He's doomed.'

– Harry Guggenheim, millionaire aviation enthusiast, 1927. Shortly afterwards Lindbergh made the first solo non-stop transatlantic flight.

'Just a fad, a passing fancy.'

– Chicago Cubs owner Phil Wrigley in 1935, about night baseball. A half-century later, after most baseball games had been played at night for years, lights were finally installed at Wrigley Field.

'I think there is a world market for maybe five computers.'

– Thomas Watson, IBM chairman, 1943

'The bomb will never go off. I speak as an expert in explosives.'

– Admiral William Leahy, chief of staff for President Truman's administration, in April 1945, four months before the bomb was dropped on Hiroshima.

'Computers in the future may weigh no more than 1.5 tons.'

– *Popular Mechanics* magazine, 1949

'Man will never reach the moon regardless of all future scientific advances.'

– Dr Lee DeForest, inventor of the audion tube and 'father' of radio, in the *New York Times,* February 1957.

'There is no reason anyone would want a computer in their home.'

– Ken Olsen, president, CEO, and founder of Digital Equipment, 1977.

'So we went to Atari and said, "Hey, we've got this amazing thing, even built with some of your parts, and what do you think about funding us? Or, we'll give it to you. We just want to do it. Pay our salary, and we'll come work for you." And they said, "No." So then we went to Hewlett Packard, and they said, "Hey, we don't need you. You haven't got through college yet."'

– Apple Computer founder Steve Jobs, recalling his and Steve Wozniak's attempts to find corporate interest in their personal computer.

'640K ought to be enough for anybody.'

– Bill Gates, Microsoft founder, 1981

'Nuclear plants, like color TV sets, give off minute amounts of radiation.'

– A 1979 *Newsweek* column by George Will, scoffing at the idea of a nuclear accident like the one in a new film, *The China Syndrome*. Will suggested the movie was hysterical propaganda from Hollywood. The next day, the Three Mile Island nuclear facility in Pennsylvania broke down, nearly killing thousands of people, an accident even more serious that the one in the movie. George Will regularly appears on television now, so don't be so sure about that colour TV set either.

'Approximately eighty per cent of our air pollution stems from hydrocarbons released by vegetation. So let's not go overboard in setting and enforcing tough emissions standards for man-made sources.'

– Presidential candidate Ronald Reagan, September 1980, in *Sierra* magazine.

Business

Icons of the industrial world have been known to make mistakes. But they know boldness is what makes businesses grow.

Writer Mark Twain just said no to an 1876 opportunity to invest $5,000 in Alexander Graham Bell's new telephone company. Instead, Twain backed another inventor with $250,000 for a new typesetting machine. The Paige typesetting machine proved to make the typesetting process more complicated, however, and the venture failed. Twain was forced to declare bankruptcy in 1894, by which time Bell's invention had started one of the most successful companies in history.

In 1886, prospector Sors Hariezon sold his gold claim in South Africa for twenty dollars. The mines on and near his claim have since yielded more than a thousand tons of gold every year, about 70 per cent of the world's gold supply.

Russian psychologist Ivan Petrovich Pavlov became famous for proving a dog could be conditioned to salivate at the ring of a bell, and won the Nobel Prize for medicine in 1904. It is less known that Pavlov tried to market his discovery by bottling dog saliva and selling it as an appetite stimulant. Humans could not be conditioned quite so easily.

'The wireless music box has no imaginable commercial value. Who would pay for a message to be sent to no one in particular?'

– 1915 response to David Sarnoff, when he urged his telegraph associates to invest in new radio technology. Sarnoff eventually found support elsewhere and helped found RCA in 1919.

'Bite the wax tadpole.'

– The original name of Coca-Cola when it was introduced in China in 1920. The company had selected a name with Chinese characters that sounded most like 'Coca-Cola'. The words sounded like Coca-Cola, but to a Chinese they had another meaning. The soda company soon changed its Chinese name, using new characters that translated as 'happiness in the mouth'.

'Stocks have reached what looks like a permanently high plateau.'

– Irving Fisher, Yale University professor of economics, 17 October 1929.

'You bought yourself a cripple.'

– New York Giants manager Bill Terry in 1935, berating farm team director George Weiss for signing a young rookie named Joe DiMaggio, because the player had an injured knee.

'I have travelled the length and breadth of this country and talked with the best people, and I can assure you that data processing is a fad that won't last out the year.'

– Editor in charge of business books at Prentice Hall, 1957.

'The concept is interesting and well formed but in order to earn better than a C, the idea must be feasible.'

– A business professor at Yale University in 1966, on Fred Smith's senior thesis outlining a reliable overnight delivery service. Smith later founded Federal Express.

'With over fifty cars already on sale in the United States, the Japanese auto industry is not likely to carve out a big share of the market for itself.'

– *Business Week*, 1968. Within a decade, Japanese cars had carved a huge chunk out of American car sales, thanks to their superb fuel economy and a world oil crisis.

In 1975, Mattel launched the new dolls 'Growing Up Skipper' and 'Growing Up Ginger', whose breasts grew when their arms were turned. The dolls with inflatable implants were an immediate flop, although collectors today now get up to $200 for one of these dolls.

'The Internet will collapse within a year.'

– Bob Metcalf, founder of 3Com Corporation, in *Info-World* magazine, December 1995. A year later, networking pioneer Metcalf took his magazine article, liquefied it in a blender, and ate it with a spoon.

Health and Safety

There are occasions when people who should know better sometimes eliminate their own DNA from the gene pool.

Ivan McGuire, an experienced parachuting instructor, jumped from a plane with a video camera to film his students. On the way down, he realized that he had forgotten to bring his parachute. His last words are on the video: 'Uh-oh.'

The Consumer Products Safety Commission made lapel buttons that said FOR KIDS' SAKE, THINK TOY SAFETY. Unfortunately, people soon realized the buttons could be swallowed by a child and, on top of that, the paint on the buttons had a dangerously high lead content. The Consumer Products Safety Commission was forced to recall its own 80,000 buttons.

In 1976, President Gerald Ford urged Congress to pass a $135 million appropriation bill to vaccinate the US population against an anticipated epidemic of swine flu. Luckily, the epidemic failed to appear. Unluckily, at least twenty-three people died from adverse reactions to the vaccine, which caused heart attacks and paralysis. The vaccine was discontinued.

In Ionia, Michigan, a drunken man tried to rob two gas station employees, but they could tell he was drunk and refused to give him any money. The intoxicated robber threatened to call the police. Still, they refused. So the man called the police and was arrested for robbery.

At the Mammoth Mountain Ski Resort in Mammoth Lakes, foam padding is wrapped around the bottom of ski-lift towers, to protect skiers from hurting themselves. Late one night, a group of friends hiked up a ski run call Stump Alley. The pranksters removed the foam pads from the lift towers and proceeded to use them as toboggans to ride down the mountain. While riding on one of the pads, Matthew Hubal, twenty-two, ran into a lift tower and was killed. It was not reported whether the tower he hit still had its protective foam pad.

'I'll show you how to set it off.'

– Jerry Strohmyer's last words before he bit down on a blasting cap, which a friend had been trying to detonate with a battery in a fish aquarium. Strohmyer, twenty-four, of Kincaid, West Virginia, survived the incident, but blew off his lips, teeth, and tongue. The fish were not injured.

In 1982, Phoenix resident David Grundman fired two shotgun blasts at a giant saguaro cactus, causing a twenty-three-foot section of the plant to fall on him. In a surreal duel in the sun, the severed cactus limb crushed Grundman to death.

A thirty-four-year-old mechanic named James Burns, of Alma, Michigan, needed to repair a farm truck. He enlisted a friend to drive the truck down a highway while Burns hung underneath, near the driveshaft, to observe where the problem might be. After driving for a while, the friend stopped and pulled over to the side of the road. The truck was fine, but Burns had been killed by the driveshaft.

Davis U. Farley was an anger-management counsellor in Boise, Idaho. In 1998, he confessed that he had gone 'ballistic' and raged through the home of Trudy Burke. Farley's anger management cost him $89,500 in damages.

A twenty-four-year-old Hialeah salesman was killed in Florida after he smashed his car into the central barrier on I-95. He had been travelling at 80 miles per hour while simultaneously reading a sales manual.

Tony Roberts, twenty-five, was being initiated into an Oregon rafting club called Mountain Men Anonymous. One drunken buddy attempted to hit an apple off Roberts's head with a bow and arrow, and missed. Roberts was hit through his right eye as the tip of the arrow passed through his brain and out the back of his skull. At the hospital, doctors reported that Roberts lost his eye, but he'd suffered no other injuries. The arrow was successfully removed from his brain, which wasn't even scratched. It is not known if Roberts qualified for Mountain Men Anonymous.

Computer analyst Mark Rifkin hacked his way into the systems of the Security Pacific Bank in Los Angeles, and successfully transferred $10.2 million to a bank account in Switzerland. However, the brilliant man was unable to keep his extraordinary accomplishment to himself, for a sober man's secret is a drunken man's speech. Rifkin boasted about the crime at a local bar. One of the patrons turned Rifkin in to the FBI.

A forty-eight-year-old San Francisco stockbroker loved to jog every day, so much so that his wife said he 'totally zoned when he ran'. One day in 1998, he zoned until he accidentally jogged off a 200-foot cliff, and was killed.

A twenty-two-year-old Wichita man decided to embark on a career in counterfeiting. He tried to use two sixteen-dollar bills at a local hotel. He was quickly arrested.

A thirty-nine-year-old Toronto lawyer named Gary Hoy was demonstrating to visiting law students the strength of his office building's windows. Hoy, 'one of the best and brightest' of his firms 200 lawyers, had given the demonstration before. This time, however, he crashed his shoulder through the window of the Dominion Bank Tower, and plunged twenty-four floors to his death.

Great News That Wasn't

Things we learned in the news media.

'Martians build two immense canals in two years'

– *New York Times* headline in 1911, for a story about how quickly the inhabitants of Mars were able to complete vast engineering projects.

'The "Greek Special" is a huge 18-inch pizza, and not a huge 18-inch penis, as described in an ad. Blondie's Pizza would like to apologize for any confusion Friday's ad may have caused.'

– Newspaper correction printed in the *Daily Californian*.

'*New York Times* reporter Lena Williams, who wrote a much-talked-about story last December about the small, everyday annoyances that bother the races, has been sold as a book.'

– New York Post

'Robbie Knievel, son of legendary stuntman Evel Knievel, made a world record jump by successfully launching his Honda CR500 231 feet, almost two-thirds of a football field and clearing thirty hotel limousines. The jump took place at the Tropicana Hotel, on the Las Vegas strip. Before the jump, Robbie left his trailer, kissed his dad Evel on the cheek and then soared into the record books.

'Upon finishing his jump, the young Knievel gave thanks to Jesus, who now lives in South Park, Colorado, and was present in the huge crowd, but who had, unbeknownst to Robbie, placed a huge amount of cash against Knievel actually making the jump.'

– *Backroads* motorcycle magazine

'SOCKS LOWER IN TOKYO'

– Headline from *The Times*

On 15 November 1998, the *New York Times* reported on American movie titles that were creatively translated into other languages around the globe. According to the *Times*, the Cantonese-language versions of such films were:

US	***CHINA***
Leaving Las Vegas	***I'm a Drunk and You're a Prostitute***
Field of Dreams	***Imaginary Dead Baseball Players Live in My Cornfield***
The Crying Game	***Oh No! My Girlfriend Has a Penis!***
Interview with the Vampire	***So, You're a Lawyer***
Babe	***The Happy Dumpling-to-Be Who Talks and Solves Agricultural Problems***
My Best Friend's Wedding	***Help! My Pretend Boyfriend is Gay***
George of the Jungle	***Big Dumb Monkey Man Keeps Whacking Tree with Genitals***

Batman and Robin	*Come to My Cave and Wear this Rubber Codpiece, Cute Boy*
Barb Wire	*Delicate Orbs of Womanhood Bigger Than Your Head Can Hurt You*

Several days later, a small correction was printed in the *New York Times,* noting that these were not the real Chinese titles after all, but spoofs from a website the editors had mistaken for truth. There were no regrets. However, we have not heard much lately from the *Times*'s Chinese bureau.

Two months later, Peter Jennings covered the movie topic on the evening broadcast of *ABC World News Tonight.* In China, reported Mr Jennings, *Babe* was called *The Happy Dumpling-to-Be Who Talks and Solves Agricultural Problems.* The pinnacle of decorum, Mr Jennings did not recite the other colourful titles rumoured to be popular in China. A few days later, Peter Jennings retracted the story during his evening broadcast. *Babe,* Jennings announced,

had actually appeared in China with another title: *I May Be a Pig, But I'm Not Stupid.*

'In last week's *Democrat*, some words were transposed through a typesetting and proofreading error. The paragraph that began "Occasionally circus elephants spent ninety-five per cent of their lives chained by two legs . . ." should have read "A majority of circus elephants . . ." while the paragraph that began "A majority of circus elephants go mad . . ." should have read "Occasionally circus elephants . . ."'

– Coos County *Democrat*

'Correction: Tuesday morning's Carlsbad *Current-Argus* called a charge residents pay for 911 service a "surge" charge. It is, of course, a sir charge.'

– Carlsbad *Current-Argus*

Consumer Awareness

Moving into the computer era has presented great challenges to some of us.

'Hello, the computer says to "Press Any Key." I cannot find the "Any" Key.'

– Customer calling Compaq's telephone help line. Compaq receives this query so often that they are considering changing the command from 'Press Any Key' to 'Press Return Key'.

Caller: 'Hello, I find that my mouse is very difficult to control while it has its dust cover on.'
Tech: 'Dust cover, ma'am?'
Caller: 'You know, the plastic bag that came wrapped around the mouse.'

An AST customer was asked to send in copies of her defective diskettes. A few days later a letter arrived from the customer, along with photocopies of the floppies.

Computer technician: 'I can help you with your problem. First, put the floppy disk into the drive and close the door.'

Telephone caller: 'Okay, hold on.'

(Sound of footsteps and door closing across the room.)

One Dell customer called to say he couldn't get his computer to fax anything. After forty minutes of troubleshooting, the technician discovered the man was trying to fax a piece of paper by holding it in front of the monitor screen and hitting the 'send' key.

'The computer screen says it can't find the printer. But I've moved the monitor so the computer is facing the printer, and the screen still says it "can't find printer."'

– A caller to IBM who thought the computer would 'see' the printer through its monitor.

'I pushed and pushed on this foot pedal and nothing happens.'

– A Dell Computer customer, after trying to turn on the power by using her mouse as a foot pedal.

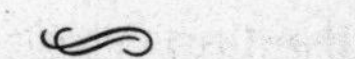

'I put in the first disk, and that was okay. It said to put in the second disk, and I had some problems with it. When it said to put in the third disk, I couldn't even fit it in.'

– An IBM customer installing new software, who had neglected to remove disks one and two, before inserting disk three. This one is not to be confused with the customer who removed the plastic casing off a floppy disk (it said to 'remove cover', after all) and tried to insert the disk's remains into the drive.

'Hello, yes, the cup holder on my hard drive broke, and my computer is still under warranty.'

– A Novell customer, who had snapped off his computer's CD-ROM drive after using it as a cup holder for several months.

Public Figures

The more famous you are, the more people appreciate your errors.

'Mr Lincoln is already beaten. He cannot be re-elected.'

– Horace Greeley, editor of the *New York Tribune*, on 14 August 1864, a few months before Lincoln creamed Democratic candidate General George B. McClellan.

'I tell you, Wellington is a bad general, the English are bad soldiers; we will settle the matter by lunchtime.'

– Napoleon on the eve of the Battle of Waterloo, 1815, where the French suffered a total defeat.

'Hurrah, boys, we've got them! We'll finish them up and then go home to our station.'

– General George Armstrong Custer, when first sighting a Sioux encampment near the Little Big Horn on 25 June 1876.

'Why didn't the passengers on the boat go into the watertight compartments and save themselves from drowning?'

– US Senator William A. Smith of Michigan, chairman of the Senate committee investigating the 1912 *Titanic* disaster. 'Watertight' Smith, as he soon became known across the country, maintained a firm grasp of the obvious about the nautical world throughout the hearings. In this instance, of course, the watertight compartments were with the rest of the ship, at the bottom of the ocean.

Entertainment impresario P.T. Barnum felt disgraced when his daughter Helen left her husband to marry a doctor in Chicago. In 1889, he cut her out of his will in favour of his other children, though he gave her a piece of worthless land in Colorado to keep up appearances. Helen's land turned out to be rich with mineral deposits, and she became far richer than all her siblings combined.

'The abolition of the commercialized liquor trade is as final as the abolition of slavery.'

– Auto maker Henry Ford in 1929.

'Prohibition's repeal will come when a hummingbird flies to Mars with the Washington Monument tied to its tail.'

– US Senator Morris Sheppard of Texas, in 1930, three years before newly elected President Franklin D. Roosevelt emancipated the commercialized liquor trade.

'The jig is nearly up. Now the Republicans begin to grasp the fact that they can beat him with a Chinaman or even a Republican.'

– Baltimore journalist H.L. Mencken, predicting President Roosevelt's defeat in 1936. He was elected for a second term that year, a third in 1940, and a fourth in 1944.

'The race will not be close at all. Landon will be overwhelmingly elected, and I'll stake my reputation as a prophet on it.'

– Newspaper publisher and one-time prophet William Randolph Hearst, in 1936.

'A Japanese attack on Pearl Harbor is a strategic impossibility.'

– CBS military analyst Major George Fielding Elliott, in a 1938 *American Mercury* magazine article.

'Japan will never join the Axis.'

– General Douglas MacArthur in September, 1940. The day after this statement, Japan announced it had joined the Axis.

'There is no Genghis Khan or Xerxes marching against our Western nations . . . This is simply a quarrel arising from the errors of the last war . . . We must not permit our sentiment, our pity, or our personal feelings of sympathy to obscure the issue.'

– Aviator Charles A. Lindbergh in a 1939 radio address, promoting that an American role in World War II should be on behalf of the Nazis, not the Allies.

'Dewey-Warren will be unbeatable . . . So, it's to be Thomas Edmund Dewey in the White House on January 20, with Earl Warren as backstop in event of any accident during years just ahead.'

– *US News and World Report*, July 1948.

'Dewey is going to be President, and you might as well get used to him.'

– *New Republic* columnist Richard Stroudt, October 1948.

'DEWEY DEFEATS TRUMAN'

– *Chicago Daily Tribune* headline, 3 November 1948.

'You won't have Nixon to kick around any more, because, gentleman, this is my last press conference.'

– Richard Nixon, 1962. He was elected President in 1968 and again in 1972.

In 1970, President Richard Nixon appointed Elvis Presley as an agent of the Bureau of Narcotics and Dangerous Drugs. In 1977, Elvis consumed more than 5,300 prescription pain-killers, amphetamines, and tranquillizers.

'The President is not going to leave the White House until January 20, 1977.'

– President Richard M. Nixon in July 1974, not long before he left the White House on 9 August 1974.

Genius for the Defence

Courtroom questions asked by real lawyers during actual trials. We rest our case.

'Now, doctor, isn't it true that when a person dies in his sleep, he doesn't know about it until the next morning?'

'The youngest son, the twenty-year-old, how old is he?'

'Were you present when your picture was taken?'

'Were you alone or by yourself?'

'Was it you or your younger brother who was killed in the war?'

'Did he kill you?'

'How far apart were the vehicles at the time of the collision?'

'You were there until the time you left, is that true?'

~

Q: 'She had three children, right?'
A: 'Yes.'
Q: 'How many were boys?'
A: 'None.'
Q: 'Were there any girls?'

~

Q: 'You say the stairs went down to the basement?'
A: 'Yes.'
Q: 'And these stairs, did they go up also?'

~

Q: 'How was your first marriage terminated?'
A: 'By death.'
Q: 'And by whose death was it terminated?'

Q: 'Can you describe the individual?'
A: 'He was about medium height and had a beard.'
Q: 'Was this a male or a female?'

Q: 'Doctor, how many autopsies have you performed on dead people?'

Q: 'Do you recall the time that you examined the body?'
A: 'The autopsy started around 8.30 PM.'
Q: 'And Mr Hubert was dead at the time?'

Q: 'Mr Slattery, you went on a rather elaborate honeymoon, didn't you?'
A: 'I went to Europe, sir.'
Q: 'And you took your new wife?'

Q: 'So the date of conception was August eighth?'
A: 'Yes'
Q: 'And what were you doing at the time?'

Q: 'Are you qualified to give a urine sample?'
A: 'I have been since early childhood.'

Q: 'Doctor, before you performed the autopsy, did you check for a pulse?'
A: 'No.'
Q: 'Did you check for blood pressure?'
A: 'No.'
Q: 'Did you check for breathing?'
A: 'No.'
Q: 'So, then it is possible that the patient was alive when you began the autopsy?'
A: 'No.'
Q: 'How can you be so sure, Doctor?'
A: 'Because his brain was sitting on my desk in a jar.'
Q: 'But could the patient have still been alive nevertheless?'

ARTS AND LITERATURE

Artists and their representatives frequently make mistakes. Not everyone instantly recognizes creative works of genius.

'I'm sorry, but you just don't know how to use the English language.'

– *San Francisco Examiner* editor in a rejection to Rudyard Kippling, 1889.

In William Shakespeare's play *Julius Caesar*, Act II, Scene 2, Caesar asks Brutus: 'What is't o'clock?' and Brutus replies 'Caesar, 'tis strucken eight.' The bard slipped up here: striking clocks were not invented until many centuries after Caesar's death.

'I'm a total ignoramus.'

– French novelist Émile Zola, founder of the naturalist movement in literature, in a letter to his friend Paul Cézanne, after failing the Sorbonne's oral exams in language and literature, and the entrance exams for the University of Marseilles.

In 1831, Edgar Allen Poe was a military cadet at West Point. Instructed to 'appear for a public parade in white belt and gloves, under arm', Poe did just as he was told. He showed up naked, except for his white belt, gloves, and rifle. He was immediately expelled.

'The world will little note, nor long remember, what we say here.'

– Words 140 through 151 of President Abraham Lincoln's Gettysburg Address, 19 November 1863.

'Rewrite it with another sense.'

– A book publisher rejecting James Joyce's *Dubliners* in 1907. *Dubliners* was rejected by twenty-two publishers before it finally came out from Grant Richards in 1914. The book was recently voted by Modern Library as one of the greatest works of fiction of all time.

'My dear fellow, I may perhaps be dead from the neck up, but rack my brains as I may, I can't see why a chap should need thirty pages to describe how he turns over in bed before going to sleep.'

– Book editor Marc Humblot in 1912, rejecting *Remembrance of Things Past* by Marcel Proust, who eventually published the book himself.

Lust for Life by Irving Stone was rejected by seventeen book publishers before the British publisher Longmans Green & Co. published it in 1934. Stone's novel about Vincent van Gogh sold more than 25 million copies, and became a 1956 film starring Kirk Douglas.

'Fantasy doesn't sell.'
'It has no pattern and is not practical for a child.'
'Verse doesn't sell.'

– Excerpts from rejection letters for an illustrated book, *And To Think I Saw It on Mulberry Street*, by a Standard Oil advertising cartoonist who called himself Dr Seuss. It was turned down by twenty-three publishers before Vanguard Press published it in 1937. Within a few years, Dr Seuss became the most famous children's writer of the century.

In 1938, Joe Shuster and Jerry Siegel sold all rights to the comic book character Superman to their publishers, for sixty-five dollars apiece. Their creation went on to become one of the most profitable in the world, earning millions for the publisher.

'A long, solemn, tedious Pacific voyage best suited, I would think, to some kind of drastic abridgement in a journal like *National Geographic*.'

– McGraw-Hill editor William Styron in 1947, about a true adventure story by Thor Heyerdahl. *Kon-Tiki* was rejected by twenty publishers before being published in 1950 by Rand McNally, who normally published atlases. Reviewers compared Heyerdahl to Joseph Conrad and Jules Verne, the book became a top-ten bestseller for two years and inspired an Oscar-winning documentary.

'It ain't a kid's book and it ain't an adult one. I'm sorry but I don't think you're going to find a publisher for it.'

– Simon and Schuster editor William Cole, in a 1963 rejection of *The Giving Tree* by Shel Silverstein. Harper and Row took the bait a year later, and the book went on to give pleasure to millions of readers.

'Too long.'
'Too slow.'
'Too clear-cut and old-fashioned.'
'Confusing and irritating.'

– Excerpts from some of the thirteen publishers' rejections for *Dune* by Frank Herbert. After Chilton published it in 1965, *Dune* sold more than 10 million copies.

***M*A*S*H* by Richard Hooker was rejected by twenty-one publishers before William Morrow published it in 1968. It became a runaway bestseller when it inspired a hit movie and a long-running television series.**

Writer Chuck Ross once conducted an experiment: he retyped Jerzy Kosinski's 1969 National Book Award-winning novel, *Steps,* and submitted it to professionals as his own work. The book was rejected by fourteen publishers and thirteen literary agents, who all failed to recognize the award-winning novel.

The Museum of Modern Art in New York City once hung Henri Matisse's painting *Le Bateau* upside down. After forty-seven days on display, a visiting art student pointed out the error, and the painting was flipped around.

***Jonathan Livingston Seagull* by Richard Bach was rejected by eighteen publishers before it was published in 1970 by Macmillan Inc. In its first five years, the book sold 7 million copies in the United States alone.**

The first literary agent to read *Going Home,* a first novel by Danielle Steel, told the prospective writer to go home and learn how to cook, for her book would never sell. Steel got a new agent, and in 1973 Pocket Books published *Going Home,* propelling Steel on a career that would make her one of the biggest-selling authors in the world.

That's Entertainment, Part 2

If the show must go on, so too must the blunders.

'What an awkward peasant girl she is!'

– Major Edward Bowes of MGM, in 1925, questioning the judgement of Louis B. Mayer in bringing over a Swedish starlet named Greta Garbo from Berlin.

'Look at his big, batlike ears.'

– Producer Irving Thalberg rejecting the young Clark Gable at an MGM screen test.

'Didn't you see those big ears when you talked to him? And those big feet and hands, not to mention that ugly face of his?'

– Jack Warner at Warner Bros, berating Mervyn LeRoy for wasting money on a screen test for Clark Gable.

'His ears are too big. He looks like an ape.'

– Darryl F. Zanuck, rejecting a contract for the young Clark Gable. Darryl Zanuck also found faults with, and failed to sign, new actors named Cary Grant, Errol Flynn, and Fred Astaire.

'I've tried movie work often enough to know I have nothing Hollywood wants.'

– Clark Gable, after his many rejections in the early days of Hollywood.

'Try another profession. Any other.'

– Drama instructor to would-be actress Lucille Ball in 1927.

'Can't act. Can't sing. Slightly bald. Can dance a little.'

– An RKO producer after viewing a 1928 screen test of Fred Astaire.

'Forget *Gone With the Wind*, Lou. No Civil War picture ever made a nickel.'

– Producer Irving Thalberg in 1936, to MGM boss Louis B. Mayer. Mayer turned it down all right but did not forget it. The book became a huge bestseller, and Mayer regretted his decision. Fortunately, *Gone With the Wind* producer David O. Selznick came to Mayer, two years later, for money to finish production. Selznick also happened to be Mayer's son-in-law. This belated opportunity enabled MGM to acquire a 50 per cent stake – late in the game, but better than nothing – in what would become one of history's highest-grossing films.

'So I offered Vivien Leigh the secondary role of Isabella in Wuthering Heights. She turned it down. I was astounded. I told Vivien she was totally unknown in America and that she wouldn't get anything better than Isabella for her first Hollywood part.'

– Director William Wyler, about a 1938 conversation he had with Vivien Leigh a few weeks before she landed the role of Scarlett O'Hara in *Gone With the Wind*.

'Silly and stupid.'

– Senate majority leader Alben W. Barkley of Kentucky.

'Outrageous . . . exactly the kind of picture that dictators of totalitarian governments would like their subjects to believe exists in a democracy.'

– South Carolina Senator James F. Byrnes, concurring with Senator Barkley in 1939 about Frank Capra's new film *Mr Smith Goes to Washington,* where James Stewart played a young senator who struggles against corruption in the nation's capital. Reviewers loved the film, however, proclaiming that it represented democracy in action and at its best.

Clark Gable and Spencer Tracy turned down the lead roles in *The Philadelphia Story,* feeling it was merely a vehicle for Katharine Hepburn. Louis B. Mayer forced Cary Grant and James Stewart into the roles, and Stewart won the 1940 Oscar for Best Actor.

Gregory Peck turned down the lead role in *High Noon,* because he felt the role was too similar to the one he portrayed in the *The Gunfighter.* The role went instead to Gary Cooper, whose career was on the decline in 1952. Cooper won the Academy Award for Best Actor in *High Noon,* which revived his movie star status.

'The biggest no-talent I ever worked with.'

– Decca Records' Paul Cohen, on dropping Buddy Holly in 1956, not long before Holly took off and became one of the greatest influences on twentieth-century popular music.

'Sean Connery can't play the sophisticated James Bond. He looks like a bricklayer.'

– Producers of the first James Bond movie, *Dr No*. They wanted Cary Grant or James Mason to star in the movie.

'Sean Connery is desperately wrong for James Bond.'

– Sheilah Graham, Hollywood columnist.

'You could do better.'

– United Artists executives in Los Angeles, after viewing Sean Connery's screen test for *Dr No.* It didn't take long for Connery to change these professional opinions.

'You have a chip on your tooth, your Adam's apple sticks out too far, and you talk too slow.'

– Universal Pictures executive rejecting actor Clint Eastwood in 1959.

Following the success of *Lawrence of Arabia,* Peter O'Toole demanded more money from David Lean to portray *Dr Zhivago*. Lean instead cast O'Toole's co-star from *Lawrence,* Egyptian actor Omar Sharif. The director then pursued newcomer Jane Fonda for the role of Zhivago's lover, Lara. Fonda was not interested because it would separate her from lover Roger Vadim. Fonda's agent begged her to take the part. By the time Fonda finally agreed to star as Lara, David Lean had discovered a young actress in London named Julie Christie, who got the part instead. Christie became an overnight sensation in *Dr Zhivago*.

Jane Fonda married Roger Vadim, and subsequently turned down the starring role in *Bonnie and Clyde* to make Vadim's movies *La Ronde* and *Barbarella*. Faye Dunaway became a household name in *Bonnie and Clyde*.

Roman Polanski offered Jane Fonda the starring role in *Rosemary's Baby,* but she turned it down. Mia Farrow made her 1968 film debut as Rosemary. But Polanski went back to Jane Fonda in 1974 when he was casting *Chinatown.* Fonda turned down that movie too, and Faye Dunaway benefited from Fonda's decision. When Jane Fonda turned down the starring role in *Network* in 1976, Faye Dunaway got the part once again, and this time Dunaway won an Oscar for her performance.

Tuesday Weld won good reviews as a budding actress in several films of the 1950s and 1960s. She seems to have preferred supporting roles, however. Weld turned down the starring roles in *Bonnie and Clyde, Lolita, Cactus Flower,* and *True Grit,* during which time she made films like *I'll Take Sweden* with Bob Hope and *Return to Peyton Place* with Eleanor Parker.

'I thought it was pro-war. So Mr George Scott did it. And now Mr Scott is the hot actor and I have to wait for the scripts he turns down.'

– Rod Steiger in 1972, on turning down the title role in *Patton.* The film had also been declined by Burt Lancaster, Lee Marvin, and Robert Mitchum. Scott won the Best Actor Academy Award, and *Patton* was named Best Picture.

'Ali McGraw is the biggest female star since Marilyn Monroe.'

– Hollywood columnist June Haber, 1970

When it came to casting Popeye Doyle in *The French Connection*, the producers faced a great challenge. The leading role was turned down by Steve McQueen, Paul Newman, Jackie Gleason, Robert Mitchum, and even columnist Jimmy Breslin. They went with their last choice and, along the way, made a star out of Gene Hackman, who won the Oscar for Best Actor in this 1971 thriller.

Producers of *Butch Cassidy and the Sundance Kid* pursued Marlon Brando to star with Paul Newman. But Brando turned it down, so the role of Sundance went to the little-known actor named Robert Redford, who became an international sex symbol.

'I was at Paramount all day yesterday, and they want me to direct this hunk of trash. I don't want to do it. I want to do art films.'

– Francis Ford Coppola to his father, in 1970, about *The Godfather* by Mario Puzo. Coppola senior talked his son into accepting the job. The movie went on to win several Academy Awards and become one of the greatest movies on the century.

Actor James Caan turned down starring roles in a string of box-office hits, including *M*A*S*H*, Love Story, One Flew over the Cuckoo's Nest, Superman,* and *Kramer vs Kramer.*

'It's unreleasable! You boys let me down.'

– Universal executive Ned Tanen, to newcomers George Lucas and Francis Ford Coppola in 1973, about their film *American Graffiti*. It was released anyway, praised by reviewers, and became a tremendously popular success. Just the same, Universal turned down Lucas's next project. *Star Wars* was picked up by Twentieth Century Fox, and it became one of the most popular films of all time.

Marlon Brando was offered the lead in *One Flew over the Cuckoo's Nest,* and turned it down. The producers recruited Jack Nicholson instead, and the entire production swept the 1975 Academy Awards, winning Best Actor, Best Actress, Best Director, and Best Picture.

Faye Dunaway acted in some great movies that Jane Fonda turned down. Later, both Fonda and Dunaway rejected the starring role in a 1979 movie based on a true story, *Norma Rae*. Martin Ritt was forced to cast Sally Field who, until then, was best known as the bubbly television star of *Gidget* and *The Flying Nun*. *Norma Rae* transformed Sally Field into a movie star, and she won the Academy Award for Best Actress.

After his enormous success as Tony Manero in *Saturday Night Fever,* John Travolta was offered leading roles in *Days of Heaven, Amercian Gigolo,* and *An Officer and A Gentleman.* Travolta turned down these roles, which precipitated a fifteen-year dry spell for the actor. These three films turned little-known actor Richard Gere into a box-office giant.

The comedy film *Arthur* was conceived with actor George Segal in the title role, but he wouldn't do the film. Segal made *Carbon Copy* instead, and *Arthur* became a 1981 touchstone for the lesser-known comedian Dudley Moore.

Robert Redford was cast as Frank Galvin, the alcoholic, ambulance-chasing attorney in Sidney Lumet's 1982 drama, *The Verdict.* Redford felt Galvin should be portrayed as a family man, and tinkered with the role so much that the producers fired him. The part was then filled by Paul Newman, who delivered a tour-de-force performance and an unforgettable character.

Debra Winger turned down leading roles in *Raiders of the Lost Ark, Bull Durham, The Fabulous Baker Boys,* and *A League of Their Own.* She chose instead to star in the movies *Betrayed, Everybody Wins,* and *The Sheltering Sky.*

Dustin Hoffman backed out of the 1982 film *Blade Runner,* which allowed Harrison Ford his first major movie outside of *Star Wars. Blade Runner* made Ford a superstar and the film remains a huge cult hit.

Actors Mickey Rourke and Sylvester Stallone turned down *48 Hours,* which teamed Nick Nolte with Eddie Murphy instead.

Anthony Hopkins turned down the role of *Gandhi* in 1982, for which Ben Kingsley won the Academy Award for Best Actor.

'When I think of all the money Whoopi Goldberg made on *Sister Act*, I want to kill myself.'

– Actress Bette Midler, who turned down the nun comedy to make *For the Boys*, a huge box-office disaster.

'I promised Hal Needham that I'd star in *Stroker Ace*.'

– Burt Reynolds, on why he didn't star in the 1983 film *Terms of Endearment*. Writer and director James L. Brooks had created a character especially for Reynolds – the washed-up astronaut named Garrett Breedlove who romances Shirley MacLaine. Some say Reynolds did not want to play an ageing astronaut with the wrong stuff. *Terms* won five Oscars, including one for Jack Nicholson in the role that had been written for Burt Reynolds. *Stroker Ace* did not win any awards.

'Bloomingdale's wouldn't work if it carried every kind of clothing ever made.'

– MTV founder Bob Pittman, on the cable channel's efforts to appeal to a white audience. In the early days MTV programming included very few videos by black artists, following the adult-oriented radio format typical of 1981: Phil Collins, Hall & Oats, etc. When MTV was several months old, CBS Records released Michael Jackson's album *Thriller,* which immediately sold 2 million copies. Groundbreaking videos were produced for 'Billie Jean' and 'Beat It'. Not everyone agrees on who got Michael Jackson on MTV (the cable company or the record promoters), but everyone agrees that it changed the future of the music channel, which is now most supportive of black artists.

Geena Davis, who stepped on to the pitcher's mound to replace Debra Winger in *A League of Their Own,* turned down *My Cousin Vinny.* The role went to newcomer Marisa Tomei, who won an Academy Award for her performance.

'The Lord is going to call me back to Heaven.'

– Television evangelist Oral Roberts in 1987, telling his followers that if they didn't send him 8 million dollars in donations, he was going to die. Roberts fell far short of his goal but he has, thus far, outlived God's death threat.

Bibliography

Altman, Diana. *Hollywood East: Louis B. Mayer and the Origins of the Studio System.* New York: Birch Lane Press, 1992.

Base, Ron. *'If the Other Guy Isn't Jack Nicholson, I've Got the Part': Hollywood Tales of Big Breaks, Bad Luck and Box Office Magic.* Chicago: Contemporary Books, 1994.

Cerf, Christopher, and Victor Navasky. *The Experts Speak: The Definitive Compendium of Authoritative Misinformation.* New York: Pantheon Books, 1984.

Farber, Stephen, and Mark Green. *Hollywood Dynasties.* New York, Putnam, 1984.

Hay, Peter. *Movie Anecdotes.* New York, Oxford University Press, 1990.

Higham, Charles. *Merchant of Dreams: Louis B. Mayer, MGM and the Secret Hollywood.* New York: Donald I. Fine, 1993.

Lawyer Journal, Massachusetts Bar Association, May 1996.

Lewis, Tom. *Empire of the Air: The Men Who Made Radio.* New York: HarperCollins, 1991.

Mank, Gregory W. *Karloff and Lugosi: The Story of a Haunting Collaboration.* Jefferson, NC: McFarland & Co., 1990.

Marsh, Dave, and James Bernard. *The New Book of Rock Lists.* New York: Simon & Schuster, 1994.

Memphis Business Journal, 'Street Talk', 9 October 1995.

Nelson, Craig. *Bad TV: The Very Best of the Very Worst.* New York: Dell, 1995.

New Yorker, 31 March 1997, 21 and 28 September 1998, 28 December 1998.

Shaw, Karl. *The Mammoth Book of Tasteless Lists.* New York: Carroll & Graf, 1998.

Smith, Joe. *Off the Record: An Oral History of Popular Music.* New York: Warner, 1988.

Wallace, Wallechinsky, Wallace and Wallace. *The Book of Lists #2.* New York: Morrow, 1977.

Wallace, Wallechinsky, Wallace and Wallace. *The Book of Lists.* New York: Morrow, 1980.

Wall Street Journal, 11 March 1999.

Now you can order superb titles directly
From Michael O'Mara Books

Please send me: *(tick boxes below)*		*Price per copy Including postage (UK only)*
☐ *Outrageous Expressions*	1 85479 556 2	£3.99
☐ *Stupid Things Men Do*	1 85479 564 3	£3.99
☐ *The World's Stupidest Laws*	1 85479 549 X	£3.99
☐ *The World's Stupidest Signs*	1 85479 555 4	£3.99
☐ *Stupid Movie Lines*	1 85479 497 3	£3.99
☐ *Women's Lip*	1 85479 524 4	£3.99
☐ *Strange Tails*	1 85479 526 0	£4.99
	Total	________

Postage and packing rates outside the UK:
Europe: add 20% of retail price; rest of world: add 30% of retail price
To order any of the above or any other Michael O'Mara titles,
Please call our credit card order line or fill in this coupon
And post/fax to:

Michael O'Mara Books
250 Western Avenue, London W3 6EE, UK
Telephone: 020 8324 5652 Facsimile: 020 8324 5678

Payment details:

Cheque: I enclose a cheque payable to MOM Bookshop Ltd for £

Credit card:

Please charge £_____ to my ☐ Access ☐ Visa ☐ Delta ☐ Switch

Card number: ☐☐☐☐☐☐☐☐☐☐☐☐☐☐☐☐

Expiry date: ____________________

Switch Issue No: ____________________

Name (BLOCK letters please): ____________________

Address: ____________________

____

Postcode: ____________________

Telephone: ____________ Signature: ____________